THE GREATER THAN, LESS THAN AND EQUAL TO

WORKSHEET

MATH BOOKS FIRST GRADE CHILDREN'S MATH BOOKS

BABY PROFESSOR

EDUCATION KIDS

Less than 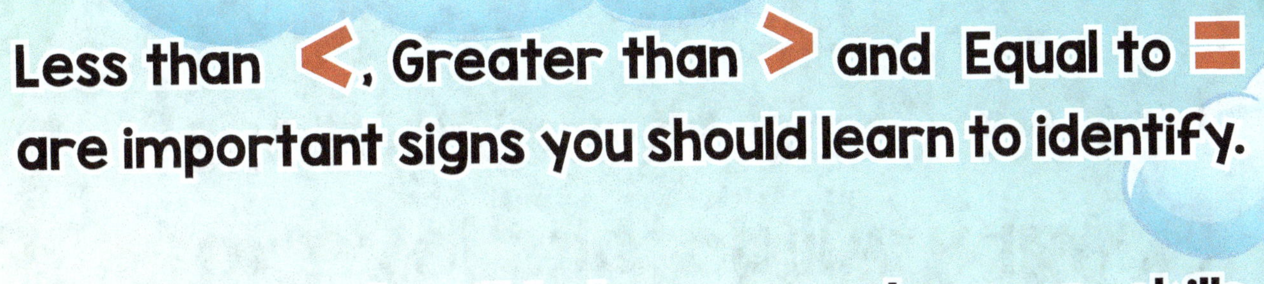 , Greater than > and Equal to = are important signs you should learn to identify.

This workbook will help you master your skills of comparing numbers and objects. Have fun and Enjoy!

Let us feed the alligators!
Hungry Alligators love to
eat the biggest numbers.

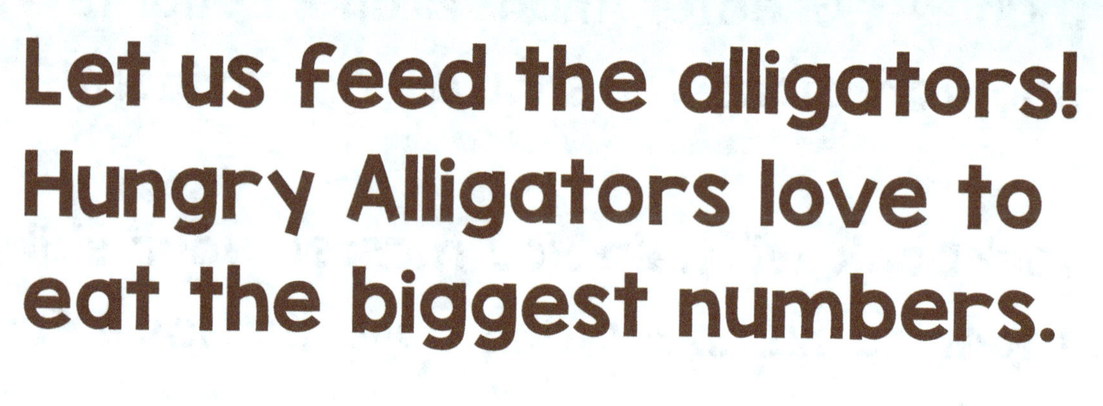

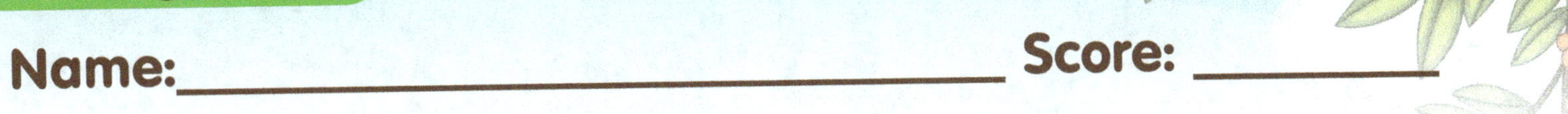

Name:_______________________ **Score:** _______

Cut out the alligators and paste them in the boxes below to solve the problems.

1. **15** [ ] **52**   5. **65** [ ] **32**

2. **88** [ ] **96**   6. **99** [ ] **67**

3. **11** [ ] **25**   7. **35** [ ] **25**

4. **62** [ ] **45**   8. **98** [ ] **14**

For cutting purposes

Name:_______________________________ **Score:** _________

Cut out the alligators and paste them in the boxes below to solve the problems.

1. **76** [ ] **83**
2. **32** [ ] **85**
3. **75** [ ] **93**
4. **48** [ ] **33**

5. **67** [ ] **99**
6. **91** [ ] **86**
7. **85** [ ] **73**
8. **79** [ ] **31**

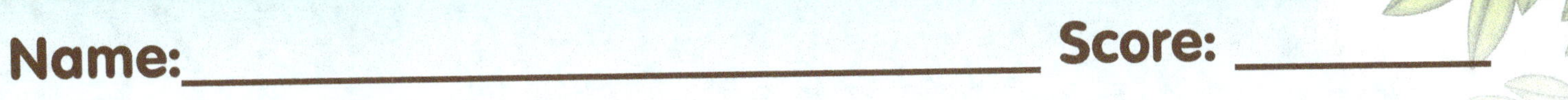

Name: _________________________ **Score:** _________

Cut out the alligators and paste them in the boxes below to solve the problems.

1. 58 [ ] 64
2. 25 [ ] 41
3. 92 [ ] 56
4. 59 [ ] 77

5. 72 [ ] 68
6. 82 [ ] 20
7. 64 [ ] 68
8. 80 [ ] 86

For cutting purposes

Activity 4

Name: _________________________ **Score:** _______

Cut out the alligators and paste them in the boxes below to solve the problems.

1. **74** ☐ **55**

2. **43** ☐ **28**

3. **91** ☐ **79**

4. **42** ☐ **38**

5. **63** ☐ **15**

6. **74** ☐ **30**

7. **60** ☐ **11**

8. **60** ☐ **18**

For cutting purposes

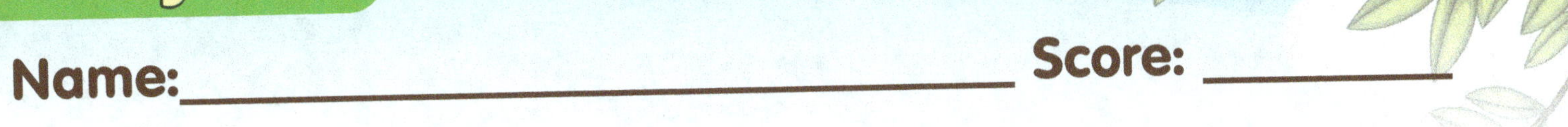

Name: _______________________________ Score: _________

Cut out the alligators and paste them in the boxes below to solve the problems.

1. 65 ☐ 68
2. 90 ☐ 14
3. 47 ☐ 62
4. 82 ☐ 96

5. 59 ☐ 88
6. 57 ☐ 80
7. 24 ☐ 39
8. 40 ☐ 63

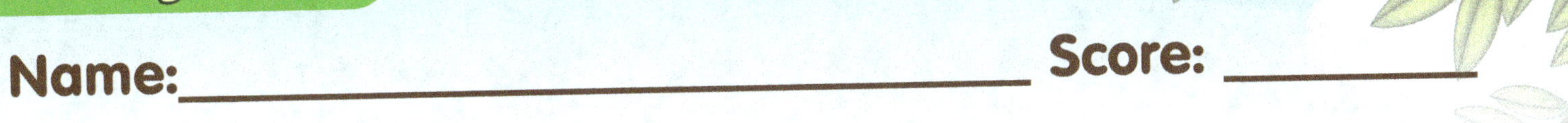

Name: _______________________________ Score: _______

Cut out the alligators and paste them in the boxes below to solve the problems.

1. **78** [ ] **77**

2. **55** [ ] **84**

3. **24** [ ] **87**

4. **99** [ ] **87**

5. **96** [ ] **93**

6. **66** [ ] **24**

7. **48** [ ] **91**

8. **35** [ ] **93**

For cutting purposes

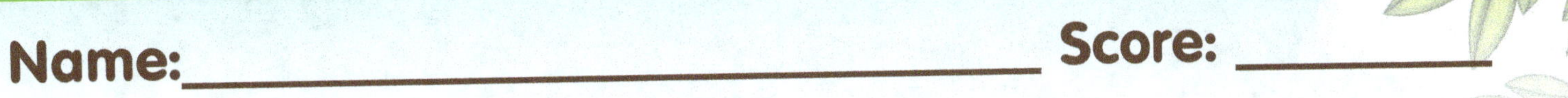

Activity 7

Name: _______________________________ **Score:** _______

Cut out the alligators and paste them in the boxes below to solve the problems.

1. 58 ☐ 66
2. 81 ☐ 13
3. 20 ☐ 86
4. 59 ☐ 37

5. 38 ☐ 79
6. 19 ☐ 16
7. 42 ☐ 22
8. 49 ☐ 68

For cutting purposes

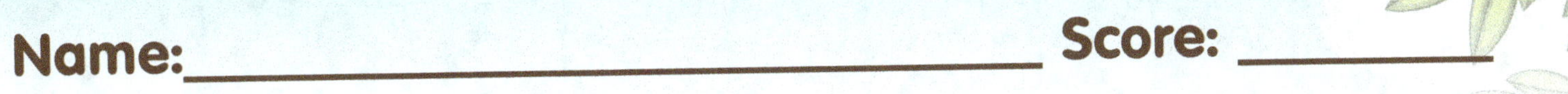

Activity 8

Name: ________________________ **Score:** ________

Cut out the alligators and paste them in the boxes below to solve the problems.

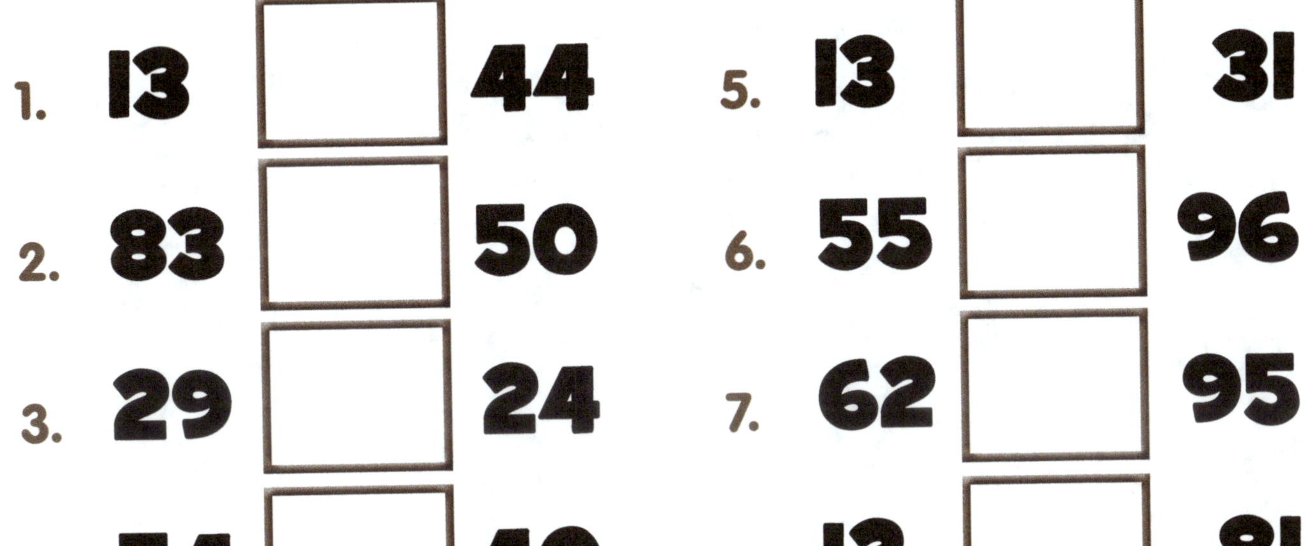

1. 13 ☐ 44
2. 83 ☐ 50
3. 29 ☐ 24
4. 54 ☐ 40

5. 13 ☐ 31
6. 55 ☐ 96
7. 62 ☐ 95
8. 12 ☐ 81

For cutting purposes

Name: _______________________ **Score:** _________

Cut out the alligators and paste them in the boxes below to solve the problems.

1. 27 ☐ 57
2. 15 ☐ 43
3. 30 ☐ 32
4. 99 ☐ 97

5. 40 ☐ 84
6. 66 ☐ 80
7. 42 ☐ 41
8. 66 ☐ 19

Name:___________________________ **Score:** _______

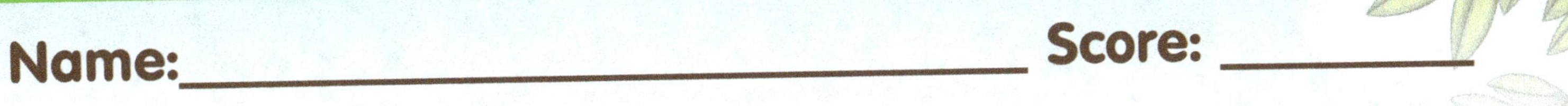

Cut out the alligators and paste them in the boxes below to solve the problems.

1. 17 ☐ 13

2. 97 ☐ 26

3. 75 ☐ 60

4. 12 ☐ 44

5. 64 ☐ 65

6. 57 ☐ 87

7. 60 ☐ 80

8. 36 ☐ 85

For cutting purposes

Name: ______________________   **Score:** __________

Cut out the alligators and paste them in the boxes below to solve the problems.

1. 61 ☐ 87
2. 20 ☐ 30
3. 40 ☐ 69
4. 55 ☐ 59

5. 40 ☐ 34
6. 43 ☐ 41
7. 19 ☐ 93
8. 37 ☐ 83

For cutting purposes

Name: _______________________________   Score: _________

Cut out the alligators and paste them in the boxes below to solve the problems.

1. 73 [ ] 42   5. 14 [ ] 79

2. 29 [ ] 78   6. 74 [ ] 79

3. 75 [ ] 34   7. 12 [ ] 76

4. 73 [ ] 70   8. 17 [ ] 57

For cutting purposes

Name: ___________________________ Score: ___________

Cut out the alligators and paste them in the boxes below to solve the problems.

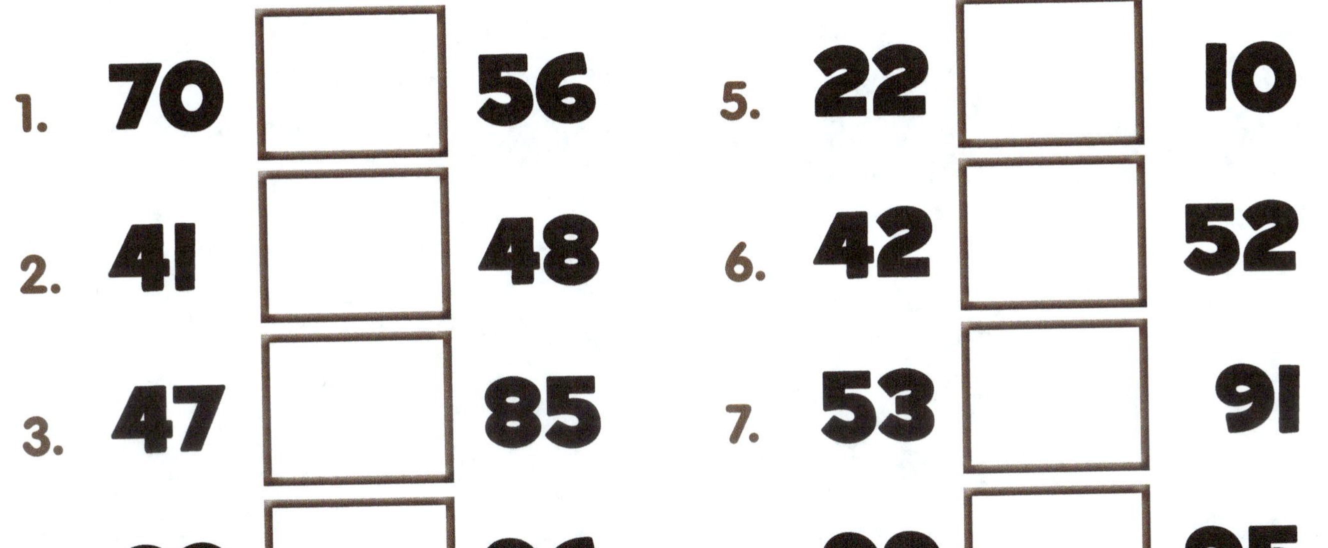

1. 70 ☐ 56

2. 41 ☐ 48

3. 47 ☐ 85

4. 83 ☐ 96

5. 22 ☐ 10

6. 42 ☐ 52

7. 53 ☐ 91

8. 99 ☐ 95

Name: _______________________________ Score: _________

Cut out the alligators and paste them in the boxes below to solve the problems.

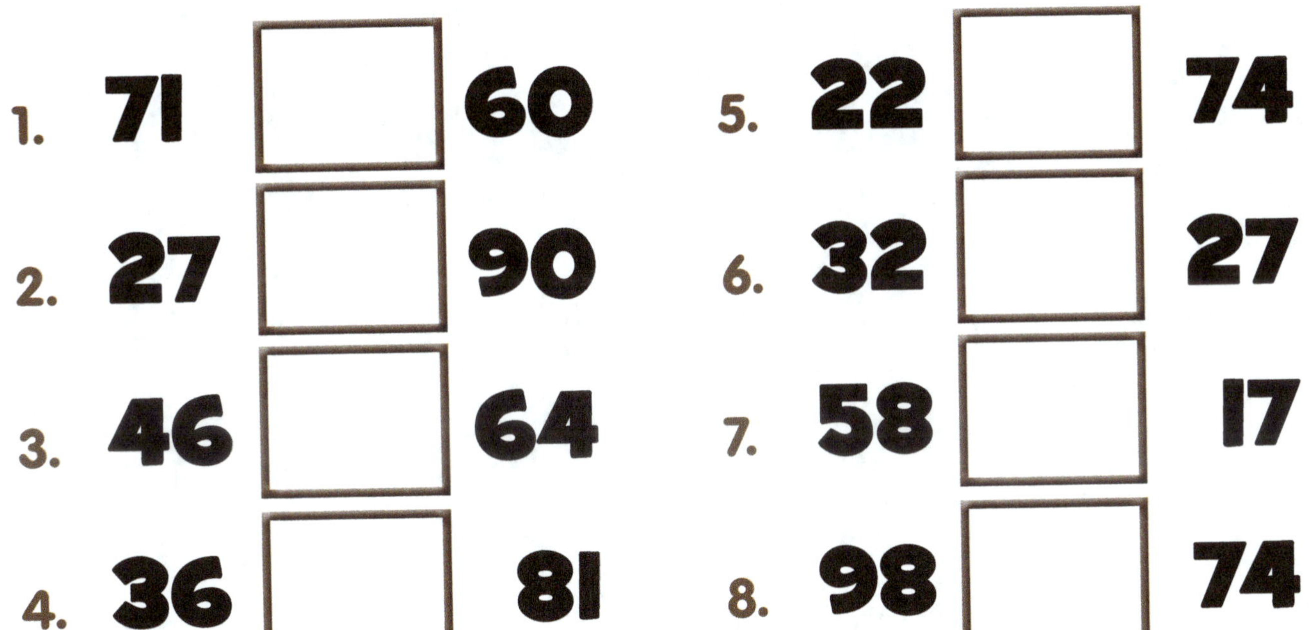

1. 71 ☐ 60

2. 27 ☐ 90

3. 46 ☐ 64

4. 36 ☐ 81

5. 22 ☐ 74

6. 32 ☐ 27

7. 58 ☐ 17

8. 98 ☐ 74

For cutting purposes

Name: _______________________ **Score:** _______

Cut out the alligators and paste them in the boxes below to solve the problems.

1. 16 ☐ 39
2. 40 ☐ 12
3. 43 ☐ 52
4. 27 ☐ 43

5. 10 ☐ 83
6. 31 ☐ 28
7. 68 ☐ 85
8. 75 ☐ 44

For cutting purposes

Name:________________________ Score:__________

Cut out the alligators and paste them in the boxes below to solve the problems.

1. 90 ☐ 67
2. 20 ☐ 33
3. 64 ☐ 99
4. 93 ☐ 52

5. 26 ☐ 95
6. 77 ☐ 55
7. 34 ☐ 38
8. 47 ☐ 77

For cutting purposes

Activity 17

Name:_______________________________ Score:_________

Cut out the alligators and paste them in the boxes below to solve the problems.

1. 15 ☐ 36

2. 27 ☐ 79

3. 21 ☐ 31

4. 72 ☐ 87

5. 99 ☐ 84

6. 82 ☐ 46

7. 92 ☐ 91

8. 66 ☐ 12

For cutting purposes

Activity 18

Name: ____________________ Score: ________

Cut out the alligators and paste them in the boxes below to solve the problems.

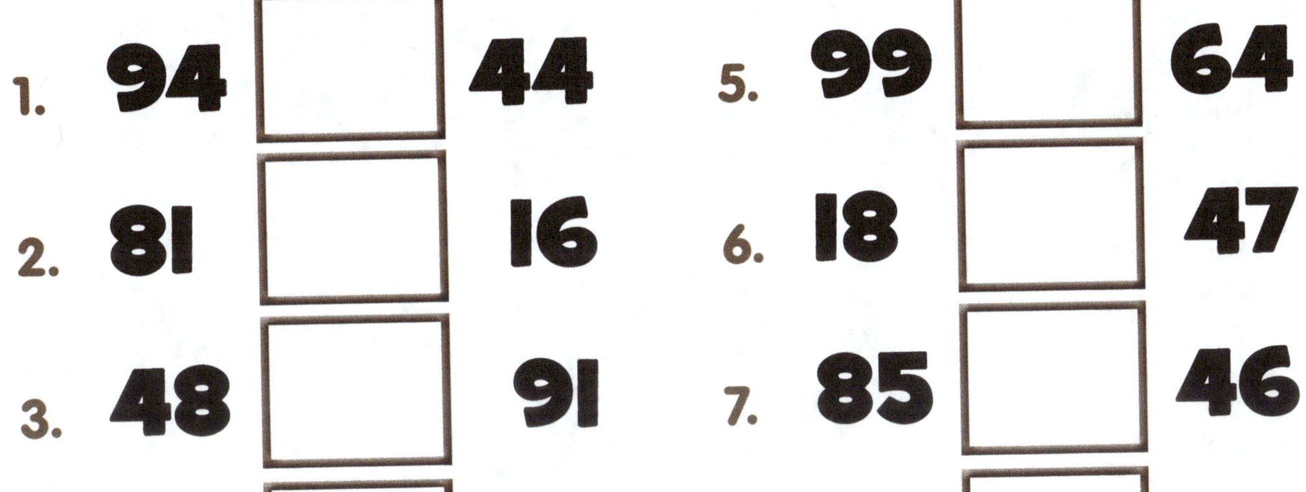

1.	94		44
2.	81		16
3.	48		91
4.	61		64
5.	99		64
6.	18		47
7.	85		46
8.	61		44

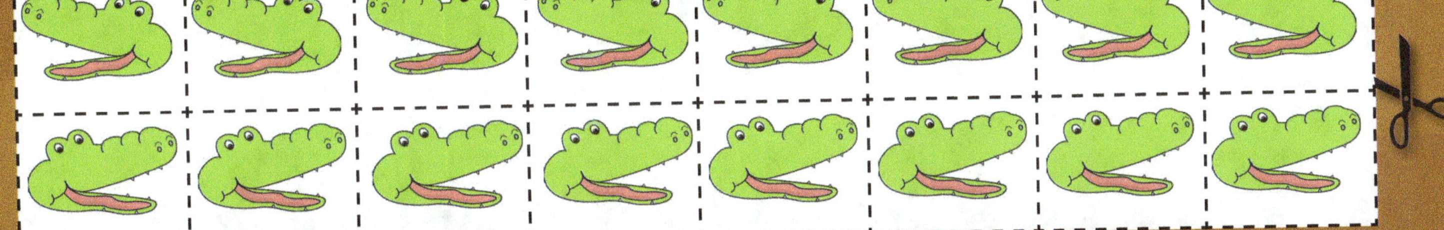

For cutting purposes

Activity 19

Name:________________________ **Score:**________

Cut out the alligators and paste them in the boxes below to solve the problems.

1. 39 [ ] 77
2. 82 [ ] 79
3. 43 [ ] 30
4. 38 [ ] 55

5. 75 [ ] 42
6. 49 [ ] 28
7. 18 [ ] 70
8. 72 [ ] 97

Name: ________________________ **Score:** __________

Cut out the alligators and paste them in the boxes below to solve the problems.

1. **62** ☐ **65**

2. **62** ☐ **75**

3. **35** ☐ **39**

4. **56** ☐ **81**

5. **64** ☐ **65**

6. **55** ☐ **47**

7. **24** ☐ **45**

8. **48** ☐ **62**

Comparing Objects

Comparing Objects

Write **>** or **<** or **=** in the box.

Comparing Objects

Write **>** or **<** or **=** in the box.

Comparing Objects

Write **>** or **<** or **=** in the box.

Comparing Objects

Write **>** or **<** or **=** in the box.

Comparing Objects

Write **>** or **<** or **=** in the box.

Comparing Objects

Write **>** or **<** or **=** in the box.

Comparing Objects

Write **>** or **<** or **=** in the box.

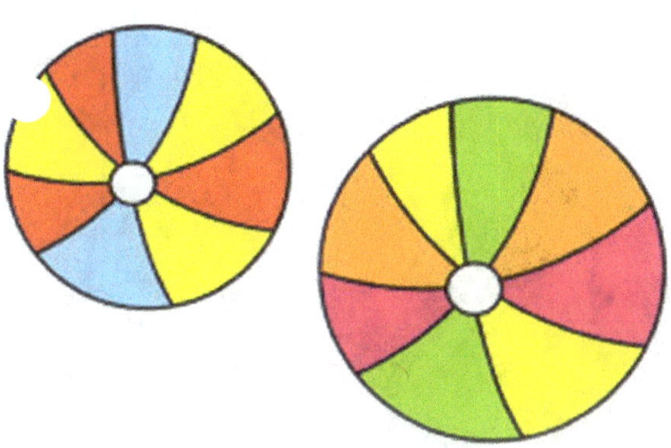

Comparing Objects

Write **>** or **<** or **=** in the box.

Comparing Objects

Write **>** or **<** or **=** in the box.

Comparing Objects

Write `>` **or** `<` **or** `=` **in the box.**

Write > or < or = in the box.

GOOD
JOB!

Activity 1

1. 15   52
2. 88   96
3. 11   25
4. 62   45
5. 65   32
6. 99   67
7. 35   25
8. 98   14

Activity 2

1. 76   83
2. 32   85
3. 75   93
4. 48   33
5. 67   99
6. 91   86
7. 85   73
8. 79   31

Activity 3

1. 58   64
2. 25   41
3. 92   56
4. 59   77
5. 72   68
6. 82   20
7. 64   68
8. 80   86

Activity 4

1. 74   55
2. 43   28
3. 91   79
4. 42   38
5. 63   15
6. 74   30
7. 60   11
8. 60   18

Activity 5

1. 65   68
2. 90   14
3. 47   62
4. 82   96
5. 59   88
6. 57   80
7. 24   39
8. 40   63

Activity 6

1. 78   77
2. 55   84
3. 24   87
4. 99   87
5. 96   93
6. 66   24
7. 48   91
8. 35   93

Activity 7

1. 58 ⬜ 66
2. 81 ⬜ 13
3. 20 ⬜ 86
4. 59 ⬜ 37
5. 38 ⬜ 79
6. 19 ⬜ 16
7. 42 ⬜ 22
8. 49 ⬜ 68

Activity 8

1. 13 ⬜ 44
2. 83 ⬜ 50
3. 29 ⬜ 24
4. 54 ⬜ 40
5. 13 ⬜ 31
6. 55 ⬜ 96
7. 62 ⬜ 95
8. 12 ⬜ 81

Activity 9

1. 27 ⬜ 57
2. 15 ⬜ 43
3. 30 ⬜ 32
4. 99 ⬜ 97
5. 40 ⬜ 84
6. 66 ⬜ 80
7. 42 ⬜ 41
8. 66 ⬜ 19

Activity 10

1. 17 ⬜ 13
2. 97 ⬜ 26
3. 75 ⬜ 60
4. 12 ⬜ 44
5. 64 ⬜ 65
6. 57 ⬜ 87
7. 60 ⬜ 80
8. 36 ⬜ 85

Activity 11

1. 61 ⬜ 87
2. 20 ⬜ 30
3. 40 ⬜ 69
4. 55 ⬜ 59
5. 40 ⬜ 34
6. 43 ⬜ 41
7. 19 ⬜ 93
8. 37 ⬜ 83

Activity 12

1. 73 ⬜ 42
2. 29 ⬜ 78
3. 75 ⬜ 34
4. 73 ⬜ 70
5. 14 ⬜ 79
6. 74 ⬜ 79
7. 12 ⬜ 76
8. 17 ⬜ 57

Activity 13

1. 70 ⬜ 56
2. 41 ⬜ 48
3. 47 ⬜ 85
4. 83 ⬜ 96
5. 22 ⬜ 10
6. 42 ⬜ 52
7. 53 ⬜ 91
8. 99 ⬜ 95

Activity 14

1. 71 ⬜ 60
2. 27 ⬜ 90
3. 46 ⬜ 64
4. 36 ⬜ 81
5. 22 ⬜ 74
6. 32 ⬜ 27
7. 58 ⬜ 17
8. 98 ⬜ 74

Activity 15

1. 16 ☐ 39
2. 40 ☐ 12
3. 43 ☐ 52
4. 27 ☐ 43
5. 10 ☐ 83
6. 31 ☐ 28
7. 68 ☐ 85
8. 75 ☐ 44

Activity 16

1. 90 ☐ 67
2. 20 ☐ 33
3. 64 ☐ 99
4. 93 ☐ 52
5. 26 ☐ 95
6. 77 ☐ 55
7. 34 ☐ 38
8. 47 ☐ 77

Activity 17

1. 15 ☐ 36
2. 27 ☐ 79
3. 21 ☐ 31
4. 72 ☐ 87
5. 99 ☐ 84
6. 82 ☐ 46
7. 92 ☐ 91
8. 66 ☐ 12

Activity 18

1. 94 ☐ 44
2. 81 ☐ 16
3. 48 ☐ 91
4. 61 ☐ 64
5. 99 ☐ 64
6. 18 ☐ 47
7. 85 ☐ 46
8. 61 ☐ 44

Activity 19

1. 39 ☐ 77
2. 82 ☐ 79
3. 43 ☐ 30
4. 38 ☐ 55
5. 75 ☐ 42
6. 49 ☐ 28
7. 18 ☐ 70
8. 72 ☐ 97

Activity 20

1. 62 ☐ 65
2. 62 ☐ 75
3. 35 ☐ 39
4. 56 ☐ 81
5. 64 ☐ 65
6. 55 ☐ 47
7. 24 ☐ 45
8. 48 ☐ 62

Comparing Objects

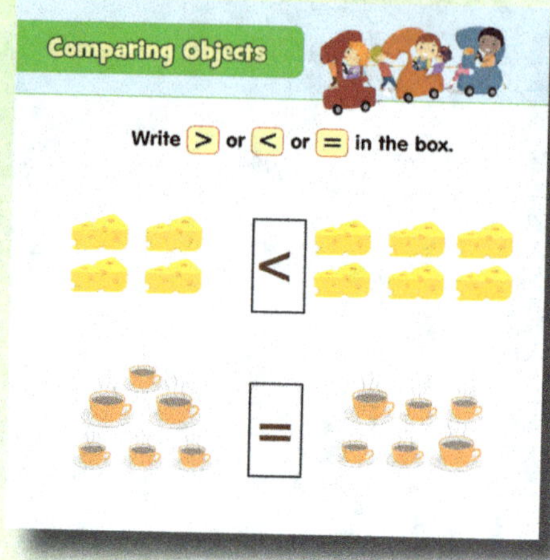

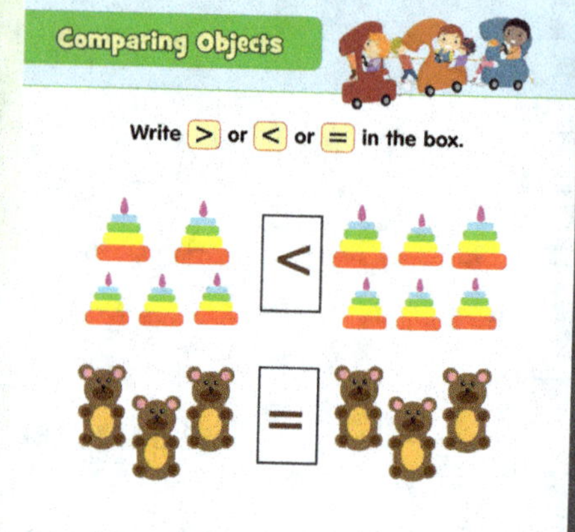

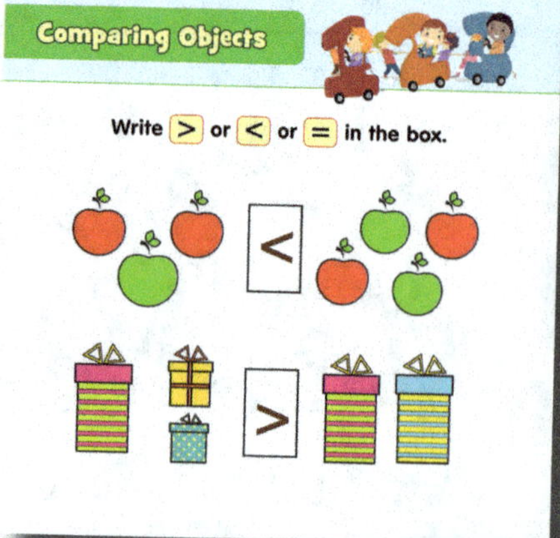

Comparing Objects
Write > or < or = in the box.
=
>

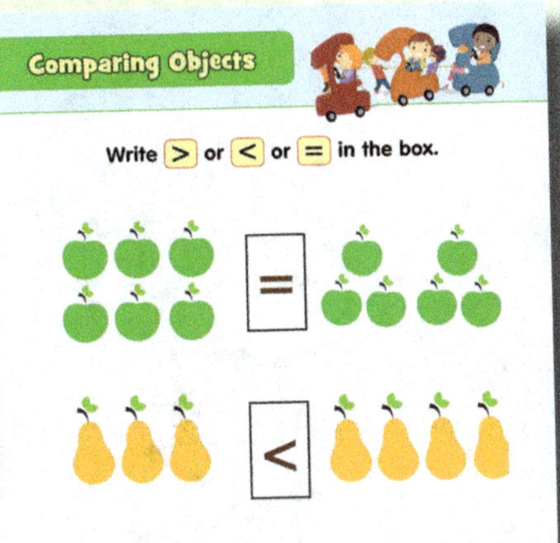

Comparing Objects
Write > or < or = in the box.
=
<

Comparing Objects
Write > or < or = in the box.
<
>

Comparing Objects
Write > or < or = in the box.
=
>

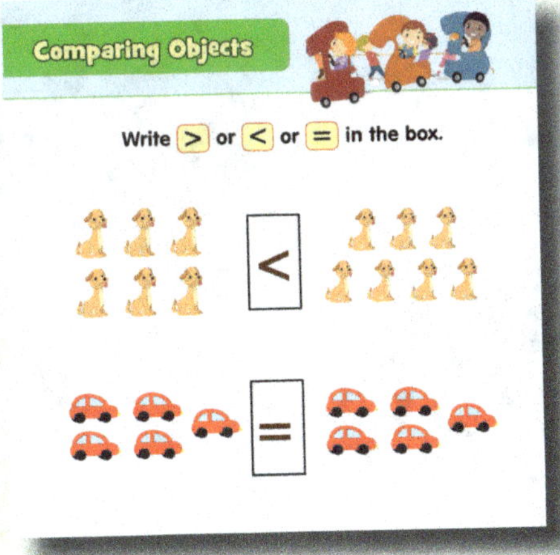

Comparing Objects
Write > or < or = in the box.
<
=

Visit
BABY PROFESSOR
EDUCATION KIDS
www.BabyProfessorBooks.com
to download Free Baby Professor eBooks
and view our catalog of new and exciting
Children's Books